SO-AZY-027

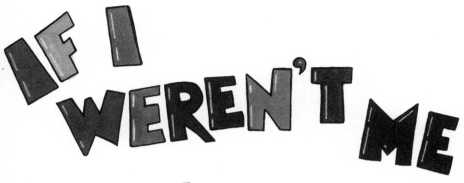

IF I WEREN'T ME

A MENAGERIE IN POETRY

HAL EVANS
ILLUSTRATED BY KEVIN POPE

Plum Street Publishers, Inc.
LITTLE ROCK

Copyright © 2017 by hal evans

All rights reserved. This book, or parts thereof, may not be reproduced in any form without permission.

Published 2017 by Plum Street Publishers, Inc.,

2701 Kavanaugh Boulevard, Suite 202, Little Rock, Arkansas 72205

www.plumstreetpublishers.com

Book design by Ponderosa Pine Design

First Edition

Manufactured in the United States of America

10 9 8 7 6 5 4 3 2 1 HC (ISBN 978-1-945268-09-0)

10 9 8 7 6 5 4 3 2 1 PB (ISBN 978-1-945268-12-0)

LIBRARY OF CONGRESS CONTROL NUMBER: 2017931900

The paper used in this publication meets the minimum requirements of the American National Standard for Information Sciences—Permanence of Paper for Printed Library Materials, ANSI/NISO Z39.48–1992.

Dedicated to the educators who sparked my imagination
and then fanned its flames with knowledge

Contents

If I Weren't Me

If I weren't me,
      what else would I be...

Something that's hidden
      or someone who's hiding?
The back that gets ridden
      or one who goes riding?

Would I do your bidding
      or spend my time biding?
It's a truly tough thing,
      this decision deciding.

A person, a place, or some other thing…
        Perhaps I'd choose *animal*,
        since I am such a fan an' all.
If I weren't a human,
        what else could I be?

Let's prowl the subject.
Let's have a look-see…

If I Were an Aardvark

If I were an aardvark,
    who'd ever see me?
Could you even spell my name right?
    And who would my friends be?

Anteaters get all the attention
    while we nose around in the dark.
Nothing ever changes. Did I mention
    they traveled topside back on the ark?

With ears of a donkey,
    the snout of a pig,
    and a kangaroo tail
    that's two sizes too big,
who wants to hug me?
    I burrow down deep
    in a mound or the ground
to chew on what bugs me,
    and weep off to sleep,
    with no one around.

It's so hard being Aard.

If I Were a Basset Hound

If I were a basset hound,
I'd be the calmest canine around.

Think you can surprise these
weary, wary eyes?
Oh, please.

If I Were an Amoeba

If I were a one-celled amoeba,
for short, my friends would call me *Ba*.
    And when I split in two
    they'd greet the new
me with, "Hey there! You must be *ReBa*."

If I Were an Armadillo

If I were an armadillo,
I'd hug the ground
when I scurried to forage
and rummage around.

I'd look both ways
before crossing the street
or end facing up
with the sky at my feet.

If I Were an Albatross

Of course I'd be cross
if I were an albatross!

What did I do? What the heck?
Why hang me around your neck?

I've never wanted a gooney thing
that doesn't float your boat.

Un-blame me for your suffering.
Make some other beast your goat!

If I Were a Bat

If I were a bat
                    a bat
                                        a bat

I wouldn't be blind,
but I'd listen for echoes
when I wanted to roam
or to wing my way home
after hunting for geckos,
insects, or fruit that I'd find—
if I were a bat
                    a bat
                                        a bat

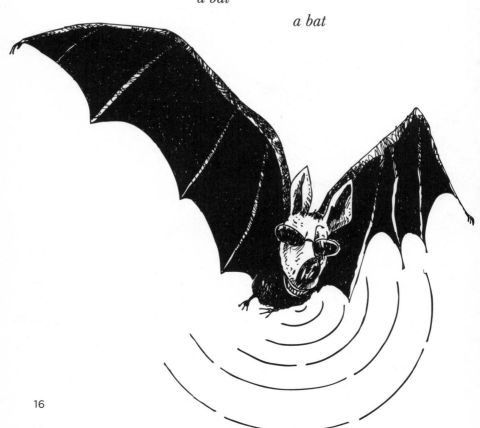

If I Were a Bull

If I were a bull,
I'd seek some help
to be absolutely certain
I wasn't full of myself.

If I Were a Bird

If I were a bird,
     sure, I'd soar up high
        and have a look around!
        Then I'd dive from the sky
     and skim along the ground
to find an open window.

Inside I'd go
     to flap and squawk
        and watch people
        scurry and swing,
        hurry and swat,
     while my cackles cracking would happily mock
their hapless and harried, horrified lot.

Then out the casement, on the fly,
     I'd sail upon a summer's breeze
        to find a perch among the trees
          and sing atop a single birch.

It is my nature to be seen and heard—
that is, it would be, if I were a bird.

If I Were a Cheetah

If I were a cheetah,
you'd know me as Abita.
But if I played fair,
you could maybe call me Cher.

If I Were a Cat

I wouldn't be—
       not a cat.
I wouldn't do it,
       and that's that.

If I Were a Clam

If I were a clam
(shy shellfish that I am!),
I'd settle for a sandy bottom
to craft my pearls of wisdom.
'Cause there, encrusted in my cloister,
the whole world would be my oyster.

If I Were a Chihuahua

If I were a chihuahua,
I'd look for my mama,
but I would not look very tall.

Then when I found her
I'd yap and hound her,
"Why did you make me so small?"

CHIPMUNK

MOUSE

CHIHUAHUA

If I Were a Jellyfish

If I were a jellyfish,
I'd ride the tide
like a bobbing party balloon,

awash with one wish—
that washing ashore I'd
find peanut butter marooned.

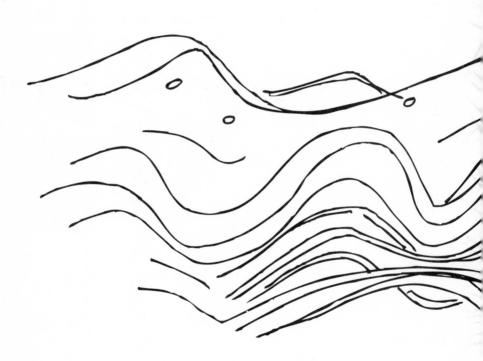

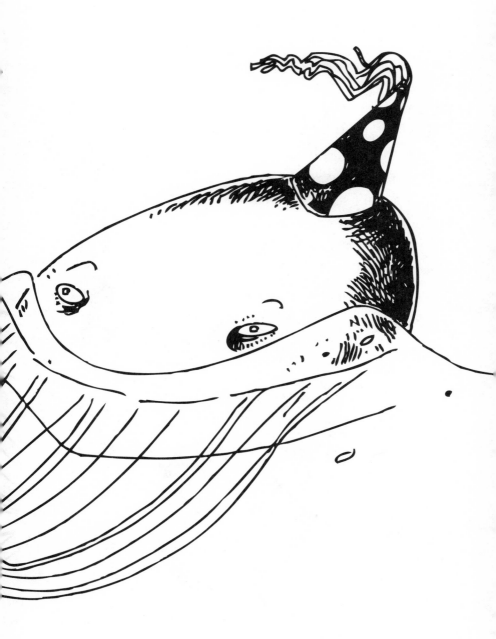

If I Were a Coati

If I were a what-ey?
I hope it's not haughty.
I hope it's not naughty.
I hope that its body
isn't too, too, too squatty.
I hope it isn't some kind o' wild polka-dotty
thing that's not even cute,
this thing called coati.
I hope it's a beaut-

                y.

I hope it a lotty.

If I Were a Dog

If I were a dog,
I'd chase away cats from the top of my my fence
who don't have the decent, common good sense
        to stay away!

I'd fetch old houseshoes
and howl out the good news
when a bone was thrown my way.

If I were a dog,
I'd locate that one itchy spot
and I'd scratch, scratch, scratch, scratch,
        scratch it—a lot.

If I Were a Gazelle

I'd hide in grass very tall, if I were a gazelle.
My horns wouldn't show at all, if I were a gazelle.

I'd leap and bound to the watering hole,
strutting my stuff with gall, if I were a gazelle.

I'd dart this way and that way with a lion's pride
close on my tail—too close to call (if I were a gazelle).

I'd catch my breath while they eat my dust!
No, I couldn't live small if I were a gazelle.

I'd live like a poem, headlong and heartstrong,
and wear a ghazal, if I were a gazelle.

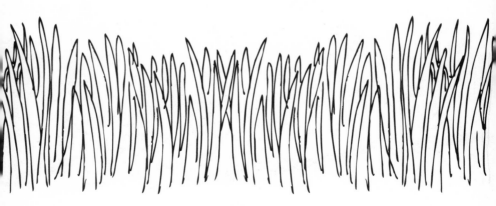

If I Were an Isopod

If I were an isopod,
I suppose I'd cross the road
to avoid being beetle food.

But the question unending,
with fourteen feet pending,
is to be or not to be shoed.

If I Were an Elephant

If I were an elephant?
That's way too wonky!
Whenever labor's involved,
I'll stick with a donkey.

If I Were a Piranha

If I were a piranha,
I'd meander
up and
down
the Amazon, a-
waiting
the encounter
of fresh friends
who swear they're gonna
dare the water…
Don't you wanna?

Come on in!
Make a splash!
Let's do dinner.
Dinner, Chicken!
Winner gets a little gnash—
O, posh!
I meant nosh.
(Oh, my gosh!)
Don't you wanna
splash and play?

I'm a piranha…
What can I say?

If I Were a Hamster

If I were a hamster,
I'd hamster in the morning,
I'd hamster in the evening,
a-runnin' my race,
spin that wheel of fortune,
tread that mill a-munchin',
I'd huff and puff, huff-a-puff in place,
and run, run, run, run, run—
run the rat race.

If I Were a Flea

If I were a flea,
I wouldn't be hiding
     in some cat's hair.
If I were a flea,
I wouldn't go riding
     'round some dog's rear.
I wouldn't suck up
     to anyone, anywhere—
     no festering follicle persisting here—
     only sweet little Pulga,
     the flea in your ear.

If I Were an Impala

I'd
Meander
Proudly
Among
Lesser
Antelopes

In
My
Prowess,
Always
Lovingly
Admired.

If I Were a Hippo

If I were a hippopotamus,
I'd be bigger than a lot of us.
But, but, but!—and this is a really big one!—
when the rains come and the rivers rise,
my belly becomes a flotation device.

If I Were an Ibex

If I were an ibex,
I could take down a T Rex!
And I've got news for that albatross…
Here's one goat you don't want to cross!

If I Were a Giraffe

It'd be no stretch to laugh
    if I were a giraffe.

What's with that neck?
    It's nearly two meters too long,
but I'd stick it out for you,
    if something went wrong.

And have you seen that tongue?
    Eighteen inches long
    by half-a-foot-wide!
Try traipsing through tongue-twisters.
    Totally! (NOT!) That's a knot
    too tough to try un-tongue-tied.

Its head is so far away from its tail
    you need two zip codes to deliver its mail.
And look at me. I'm much too tiny
    to jump up and reach that tall, speckled hiney!

I guess it won't work.
    A giraffe's not for me.
Still I bet when it sings
    it can reach a high C.

If I Were a Donkey

If I were a donkey,
　　my name would be Jack,

and if you were late with my stack,
　　or bale, or forkful of hay,

I'd lower my nose and noisily bray
　　to remind you that mealtime had passed.

And if someone inquired why you hurried away,
　　you'd stop, smirk, and tell them,
　　"Because Jack asked."

If I Were a Jackalope

If I were a jackalope,
you'd let me clarify, I hope:
Now please, don't cackle,
but I'm not a jackal.
Some have a confusing habit
of thinking, "Aha! A mutant jackrabbit!"
And let me use this little trope
to swear I'm not an antelope.
Nope.
Nope, nope.
Nope.
I am simply that that I am,
a fantastic animal afoot on the lam.

If I Were a Koala

If I were a koala,
  I'd sit in a tree
and chew eucalyptus
  while you ogle me.

I'd take my vacation
  in Kuala Lumpur
'cause that's where koalas hang out
  (I'm barely sure).

We'd let our fur down,
  get wild—whoop and holler!
Then I'd settle back like a calm, cuteness wallah.
  That's what I'd do, if I were a koala.

If I Were a Leopard

If I were a leopard,
I'd wear camouflage
so no one could spot me,
a polka-dot mirage.

If I Were an Otter

I'd dive and sputter
and float and flutter
and do a lotta water
things like I ought-er—
If I were an otter.

If I Were an Okapi

If I were an okapi,
I'd have to deal with being different,
withstand the gawking ignorant jeers—
"What are you supposed to be?"

And hear the savage bully laugh,
"Holy cow! What on earth?
Look at that freakish animal!"

And, "What is that? A short giraffe?"
And, "No, that smacks of zebra birth!"
And, "It looks to me like a messed-up camel!"

Whom am I supposed to please?
Uniquely sacred, my own species—
There is no copy
for me, the okapi.

If I Were a Marmot

If I were a marmot,
I'd hurry up to the tree line
and scurry across the alpine
in my fluffy, furry self
to pose for photos on a precipice
high atop the continental shelf.

If I Were a Mole

If I were a mole,
I'd live in a hole
and come out at night
to avoid the light.

I'd burrow down deep,
preferring to sleep
secure in my knoll,
if I were a mole.

If I Were a Zebra

If I were a zebra,
no one could touch me
as I gallivant
across the Serengeti.
Hyenas can't catch me.
they've already tried.
When cheetahs give chase
I take them for a ride.

I've earned my stripes
(all kidding aside).
If you want the secret
to stripping my hide,
drop your barking and growling,
your mewing and whines—
and get close enough
to read between lines.

If I Were a Butterfly

I'd light on your nose
      if I were a butterfly,
free to flutter by.

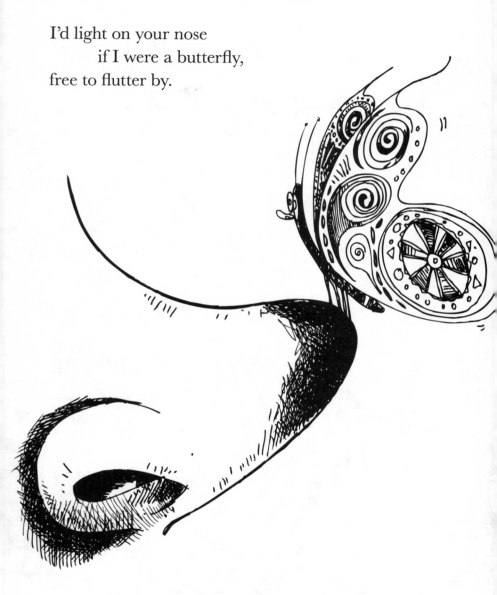

If I Were a Pterodactyl

If I were a pterodactyl,
I'd have been long since gone.
I'd have faded like fractals
with my bro, Pteranodon.

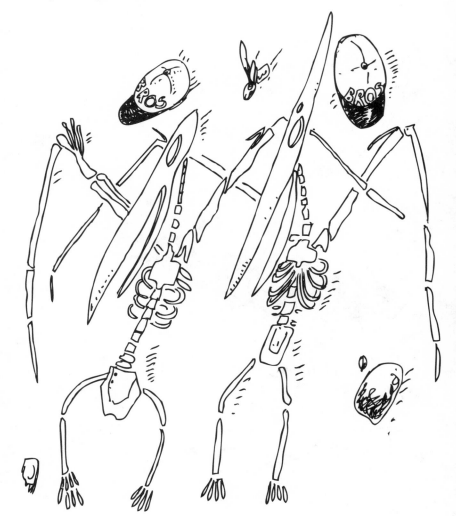

If I Were a Narwhal

If I were a narwhal,
I'd be embarrassed, y'all,
when they call me
"Unicorn of the Sea."

I'd have to laugh
and dive a mile and a half
so no one sees me blush…
"Unicorn!" Aw, hush.

If I Were an Ostrich

If I were an ostrich,
I'd hide my head.
Nothing rhymes with ostrich.
Could I choose *emu* instead?

If I Were a Lynx

If I were a lynx,
I'd tread the ground lightly
and follow my instincts
both day and nightly,
in hopes I didn't go missing.

If I Were a Snail

Slowly,
Naturally
Actually,
I
Labor,

Speeding surreptitiously,
Negotiating newfound
Avenues, as,
Inching, I
Lumber, lately,

Serenely sliding, spying,
Noting nothing necessary,
Always aspiring after
Infinitely important issues—
Laughing loudest, lastly.

If I Were a Panda

If I were a panda,
I'd chew my bamboo
all the day through
with a face photo-perfect
for bamboozling you.

If I Were a Paramecium

If I were an amoeba,
I'd be single-celled and lonely,
but a paramecium—that sounds better
than just one and only!

If I Were a Beagle

I'd frolic like the month of June.
I'd flop my ears
and flap my jowls
and bay the moon
with mournful howls.

I'd run and jump
at birds and clouds
and land—*kerthump!*—
and count my *Ow*!s
to mockingbirds' jeers.

If I were a beagle,
some days,
dog-gone it,
I might really want it—
and wish that I were an eagle.

If I Were a Pigeon

If I were a pigeon,
You'd call me a rat with wings.
I wouldn't be liked like
that cooing bird who sings.

I'd walk the streets
and beg for food
and avoid the vagrant
who mutters that I look tasty.
I'd run hastily
afoot, or flap above
to rest on gutters.

A dove gets all the love.

If I Were a Polar Bear

If I were a polar bear,
I'd dine on salmon and caviar
and floss my teeth with walrus hair.
I'd paddle the Arctic water
to kick back in the snow.
Belly up in the sunshine,
I'd go with the floe.

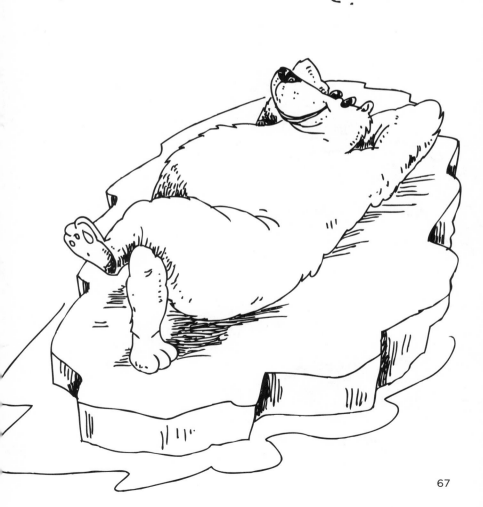

If I Were a Platypus

If I were a platypus,
      I'd waddle off to the gym,
work off a few pounds
      'til I looked really slim.

Then I'd take my friend, 'Potamus,
    to a hip restaurant.
We'd live our lives large,
    and for extra flaunt,

I'd order some duck
    and send him the bill.
If I were a platypus,
    that's how I'd keep it real.

If I Were a Python

If I were a python,
I'd hold my love tight on
a night in the jungle
and try not to bungle
how closely I held her to me.

If I Were a Quokka

I'm no average grassland wannabe—
I'm a full-fledged, pooch-pouched wallaby!
What's that? You've never heard o' me?
Of course. Okay. Whatevvah!
Quote me on this:
You can't knock a quokka.

If I Were a Viper

I would not want to harm
you with my venomous bite.
There's no need for a charm—
watch me wiggle upright.
With my Squeegee-like skin,
I can swerve across glass
unlike a furry old pet.
You'll see what I mean
when it rains—I'll surpass
the best windshield viper yet.

If I Were an Octopus

My legs would be enormous
if I were an octopus.

Waving eight times—*Hello!*—
I'd propel myself and go

whooshing and swooshing on the fly,
eight legs octo-pushing—*Bye-bye!*

Look at the time! Mustn't be late.
An octopus always arrives by eight.

If I Were a Kangaroo

If I were a kangaroo
bouncing through the outback,
I'd be a joey and trade in my pouch
for a sporty brand new backpack.

If I Were a Shark

If I were a shark,
I'd swim and smile.

I'd pass and observe
you all the while.

I'd swim up close—
swim up and swerve.

I'd grin and mark
if you had the nerve
to swim with me.

Hmm, you look like bait...

If you swim with sharks,
Don't hesitate...

Uh-oh.
Too late.

If I were a Meerkat

If I were a meerkat, living in the ground,
I'd poke up my head to sneak a peek around—WHOA!
Is something moving over there?

Okay. As I was trying to say,
If I were a meerkat, coming out to play—WAIT!
Whew! My shadow really gave me a scare.

Don't call me a prairie dog. I'm not
Some furry little rodent, I'm a meer—WHAT?!
Be still… don't blink… just… stare…

This stop-and-start stuff can really get old.
In the carnival midway, I'm whack-a moled.

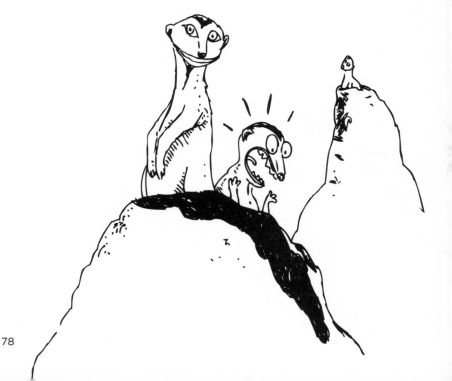

If I Were a Rhinoceros

I would not be a rhinoceros.
I'd be too heavy
to ride in my Chevy,
and a face like that is preposterous.

If I Were a Snake

I'd pitch a hissy fit
    if I were a snake.
With all of that crawling,
    wouldn't you bellyache?

Of course my demeanor
    would seem surly or mean or
    spitefully loaded with spit.
Who wouldn't slither if spawned in a pit?

I'd ask you, "Please, come hither, get closer, a bit."
    But you'd hang back for fear that I'd trick you.
"Alas," I'd say, "I suppose you should split.
    Far be it from silly ol' me to constrict you."

If I Were a Worm

If I were a worm,
I'd have to squirm,
crawling and munching
my way through the dirt.

But if I wore glasses,
take a long second look…
Bet your library passes
I'm digesting a book.

If I Were a Saint Bernard

If I were a Saint Bernard,
my name would be Shasta.
I'd winter in Wyoming
and summer in Alaska.

And when I arrived
in the snow with my keg,
you'd be the one
to sit up and beg.

If I Were a Roach

Don't be so cocky!
Who asks such a thing?
A roach is so gross
it don't need no sting!
(Roaches are so icky
even their grammar is bad.)

There's a roach in the kitchen
having a blast— Eeewww! Egad!
Quick! Turn on the light!
See it scoot away mad
'til you wham a swift swat
and that bug's RIP-ing!
  ... In cockroach heaven
  or some place like that...
  wherever they go
  when they've just made a splat.

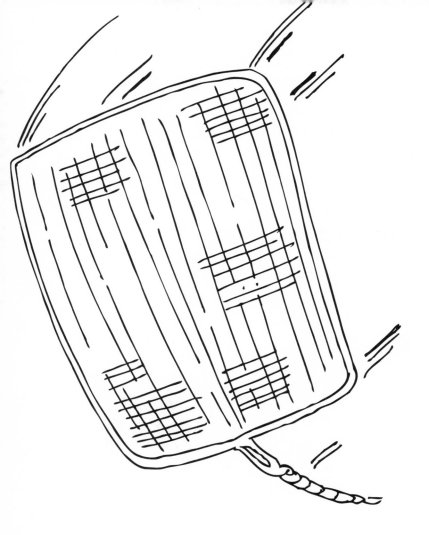

If I Were a Salamander

Naming a lizard, you see,
  requires no great wizardry.
The challenge can be met
  oh so quite easily.

As a girl I'd be Amanda,
  as a boy, Alexander,
Or possibly Lysander—
  that is, if I were a salamander.

If I Were a Sea Anemone

If I were a sea anemone,
    I wouldn't bother an otter
    down there underwater.
I couldn't be an enemy—
    not me!—a sweet sea anemone.

If I Were a Unicorn

Why would I be so hard to find?
    If I were a unicorn,
    I'd be one-of-a-kind.
How could you miss my singular horn?

I'm here.

                    Over here.

Don't you hear?

                    Oh, dear!

Why can't you see me,
    alone and forlorn?
Can anyone find me,
    a lone unicorn?

If I Were a Sloth

If I
were a three-toed
sloth, I'd move in slow mo,
like syllables crawling through drawls,
y'all … Whoa.

If I Were a Vulture

If I were a vulture,
I don't know that I'd want to be.
A vulture has carrion culture,
glaring down from a branch
o'er-perched like a critic,
hoping to catch some
poor prey in the lurch.

If I Were a Vampire

If I were a vampire,
don't think of me as scary.
I'd have two fangs
and talon nails and
of course, I'd still be hairy.

But don't worry
about the dark night,
the clouds and moon
above your head.

I'd locate something tastier—
      something sweeter—
than simply your neck to bite.

I'd swoop past you
      for dread, for fright,
      in the dead of the night,
and suck blood oranges instead.

If I Were a Snow Snake

If I were a snow snake,
I'd lie very still
on powder white slopes
to trip skiers' hopes—
unbinding each heel…

If I were a snow snake…
I mean, like, for real.

If I Were a Squid

A squid
sounds silly. I'm
calamari at best,
something lesser than octopus,
I guess.

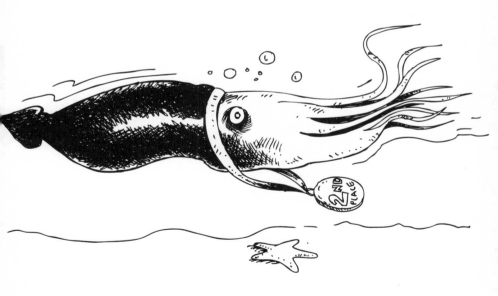

If I Were a Walrus

If I were a walrus,
I'd imagine myself a beetle,
or maybe a blackbird singing in the night,
or perhaps something perfumed with musk—
an ox or a rat might be alright.
Or… what if… maybe I'd be
a saber-toothed cheetal
on the prowl from dawn till dusk!

Oh, dear. Really?
Dear, deer. That's silly…
I'm such a walrus.
Tsk, tsk.
Kook-a-choo.
Tusk, tusk.

If I Were a Spider

If I were a spider,
I'd play the silent poet,
spinning songs in gossamer;
and, before you know it,
you're webbed and bitten
with words' softest venom. See?

It's completely written,
your poem from me.

If I Were a Scorpion

Finding me wouldn't be easy—
    Up front is not where you should look.
I'd be lurking toward the back, be-
    tween darker gutters of this book.
Be careful what you seek back here…
    Beware my stinging tell-tale fleer!
I'm not the one who ought to fear
    Whenever I bring up the rear…
        Beware,
         if I
         were
          a
         s   !
         c   n
          o o
          r p i

If I Were a Pteranodon

Perhaps it was pneumonia…
It's possible!
Or did something psychological
send me the way of my pal,
Pterodactyl?
Like a phantom appendage
pulling me toward the past,
like a useless initial,
overlooked and o'er-passed?

My psquawk was pterrifying
prior to nabbing my prey!

Now long psince psilent,
where am I ptoday?

If I Were a Tarantula

If I were a tarantula,
I'd trip the light fantastic!
I'd dance the tarantella,
so furiously fast a fellah
my legs would seem elastic!

If I Were a Tortoise

If I were a tortoise,
my mind would be a fertile place,
imagining notions at a rapid pace.
Yet one thought spans my purpose,
consuming my turtle space:

Slow and steady wins the race.

104

If I Were a Monarch

Monarch

orange   black

flitting   flying   departing

larva   chrysalis   diamond   metamorphosis

sleeping   waking   returning

magnetic   majestic

journey

If I Were an Xanthareel

If I were a xanthareel,
I know just how I'd feel—
my tastes would be eclectic!

Fusing ancient and modern cuisines,
my life would spark the stuff of dreams,
as I sing my body electric.

If I Were a Yak

It's me … in time out, again … Alack!
Busted for not-so-smart-talking back.
    It's not that I'm proud,
      but my thoughts are all loud.
That's why I'm a yakkety yak.

If I Weren't Me (Finale)

What a lot of animals!
    In vivid vast variety!
How's a person to choose?
And would I truly be happy
surrendering my words
    for barks and brays, and howls and mews?

Blackbird or crow, hare or rabbit,
    what's really in a name?
Being human suits my habit;
    it keeps my skin in the game.

So, now…
I must conclude,
    without further ado
    and not much misgiving,
of all the animals living
    I'd wish I could be,
I'd still fit in best,
    better than all the rest—
    if I were simply me.

Index: Poems by Type

Octave
Bat (16)

Quatrain(s)
Armadillo (14), Bull (17), Cat (21), Cheetah (20),
Elephant (31), Hippo (38), Kangaroo (75), Koala
(44), Leopard (46), Mole (51), Narwhal (56), Ostrich
(58), Panda (62), Paramecium (63), Platypus (68),
Pterodactyl (55), Rhinoceros (79), Saint Bernard (83),
Salamander (86), Snake (80), Spider (98), Worm (82),
Zebra (52)

Quintain
Basset Hound (12), Ibex (39), Lynx (59), Otter (47),
Python (70), Sea Anemone (87), Tarantula (102)

Sestet
Clam (22), Marmot (50), Quokka (71), Tortoise (103),
Vulture (91)

Septet
Polar Bear (67), Snow Snake (94)

Shape
Scorpion (99)

Ten Line
Flea (35), Viper (73)

Tercet(s)
Chihuahua (23), Dog (27), Isopod (30), Jellyfish (24),
Xanthareel (106)

Even the most reluctant readers will absorb poetic structure and technique through imaginative wordplay

If I weren't me,
What else would I be?

It's a universal question we all wrestle with, particularly as children. And it provides creative fodder for poetry teacher hal evans, who brings the sensibilities of Ogden Nash and Shel Silverstein, illuminated with zany pen-and-ink mashups by illustrator Kevin Pope.

Leading the reader through a poetic menagerie in which our narrator tries on different guises, evans puns and brays and marches his way through a language-arts funhouse, adopting stances ranging from droll to comical to clever.

As they engage in evans' infectiously zany wordplay, kids respond in kind, blissfully unaware that they are absorbing poetic structure, form, and technique.

 **hal evans** is a poet, playwright, actor, and teacher who serves more than 60,000 students and teachers annually. He brings curricula to life through interactive performances and workshops, including professional development addressing cross-curricular arts integration. He serves as a performance coach for Poetry Out Loud, an Artist-in-Education for Texas, Arkansas, and the Mid-America Arts Alliance, and a frequent presenter at educational and library conferences. He lives in Cypress, Texas, outside Houston.

 **Kevin Pope's** illustrations and cartoons have appeared in alternative publications, global advertising campaigns, and numerous books. His comic panel, *Inside Out*, was syndicated nationally, and those designs were also licensed for use on merchandise. As an animator, he worked as the head character designer for the NBC prime-time show *Sammy*, Mad Magazine's *Project X*, and as a content developer for DC Entertainment. He works and resides in the hills of southern Indiana.

NOV   2017